The Missions of California

Mission San Luis Obispo de Tolosa

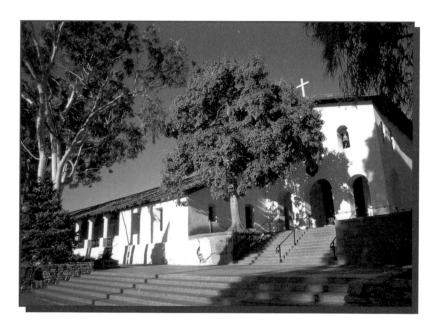

Kathleen J. Edgar and Susan E. Edgar

The Rosen Publishing Group's
PowerKids Press™
New York

Published in 2000 by The Rosen Publishing Group, Inc.
29 East 21st Street, New York, NY 10010

Photo Credits and Photo Illustrations: pp. title pg, 5, 32, 49, 51 by Christina Taccone; pp. 4, 48, 50 by Shirley Jordan; p. 7 Courtesy of National Parks Service, Cabrillo National Monument; p. 8 © Basilica of Santa Croce, Florence, Italy/Superstock; pp. 11, 14, 17, 40 by Michael Ward; pp. 12, 29, 36 by Eda Rogers; pp. 13, 34 by Tim Hall; p. 18 © Superstock; p. 20 © Seaver Center for Western History Research, LA County Museum of Natural History; pp. 21, 29, 37 © North Wind Archives; pp. 22, 25 © CORBIS/Bettman; p. 26 by Gil Cohen; p. 28 © Christie's Images/Superstock; p. 31 © CORBIS/Underwood & Underwood; p. 33 © Department of Special Collections, University of Southern California Libraries; pp. 38, 39 © The Granger Collection; pp. 45, 46 © Santa Barbara Mission Archive-Library; pp. 52, 57 by Christine Innamorato.

First Edition

Book Design: Danielle Primiceri

Layout: Kim Sonsky

Editorial Consultant Coordinator: Karen Fontanetta, M.A., Curator, Mission San Miguel Arcángel
Historical Photo Consultants: Thomas L. Davis, M.Div., M.A.
                            Michael K. Ward, M.A.

Edgar, Kathleen J.
        The Mission of San Luis Obispo de Tolosa / by Kathleen J. Edgar and Susan E. Edgar.
            p.   cm. — (The missions of California)
        Includes bibliographical references and index.
        Summary: The history of this California mission from its founding in 1772, through its development and use in serving the Chumash Indians, and its secularization and function today.
        ISBN 0-8239-5491-9 (lib. bdg.)
        1. Mission San Luis Obispo de Tolosa (San Luis Obispo, Calif.)—History Juvenile literature.
    2. Spanish mission buildings—California—San Luis Obispo Region—History Juvenile literature.
    3. Franciscans—California—San Luis Obispo Region—History Juvenile literature. 4. California—History—To 1846 Juvenile literature. 5. Chumash Indians—Missions—California—San Luis Obispo Region—History—Juvenile literature. [1. Mission San Luis Obispo de Tolosa (San Luis Obispo, Calif.)—History.
    2. Missions—California. 3. Chumash Indians—Missions—California. 4. Indians of North America—Missions—California.] I. Edgar, Susan E. II. Title. III. Series.
    F869.M665E24   1999
    979.4'78—DC21   99-21305
                                                                      CIP

Manufactured in the United States of America

Contents

The Spanish Arrive in Alta California

In the busy community of San Luis Obispo, shops, restaurants, and houses line the streets. Nestled in a downtown neighborhood is what remains of the early days of Mission San Luis Obispo de Tolosa. The church, with its whitewashed adobe and red tiled roof, towers above the nearby buildings. There are three bells over the entrance of the church. A cross on the roof peak reminds residents and visitors of the Spanish friars who came hundreds of years ago to establish 21 missions in what is now California.

Named after the Bishop of Toulouse, who was the son of a king, Mission San Luis Obispo de Tolosa is called the Prince of the Missions. The complex now spans an entire city block. Roses and cacti bloom on the inside of the quadrangle. Grape vines grow over arbors, the fruit catching the light of the sun. Lacy lemon eucalyptus trees cast gentle shadows on the white buildings. A fountain, featuring a sculpture of a California Indian child sitting beside a bear, stands near the mission. It evokes a time when the area, called the Valley of

▲

This mission fountain depicts an American Indian child sitting with a bear in the Valley of the Bears.

◀ *The number 1772 appears on the front of the church, announcing the year that the mission was founded.*

the Bears by the early Spanish missionaries and soldiers, was inhabited by California Indians.

More than 225 years ago, the rich West Coast landscape was a wilderness, virtually unexplored by white settlers. The whole coastline was populated by about 300,000 Indians. When the Spanish came to settle California in 1769, they sent soldiers and friars to build missions at San Diego and Monterey. They continued to construct settlements that were about one day's ride apart from each other, all the way from San Diego in the south to Sonoma in the north. Mission San Luis Obispo de Tolosa was the fifth mission founded in Alta California during this 30-year endeavor.

The Spanish interest in the land we now know as California began more than 450 years ago. After Christopher Columbus sailed to the lands that Europeans called the New World (North America, South America, and Central America) in 1492, the king of Spain sent explorers to learn more about these lands. In the 1500s, the Spanish sailed to California in search of gold, spices, and other riches.

Wealth was not the only reason that Spain wanted to claim the New World. The Spanish practiced Catholicism (a branch of Christianity) and believed that everyone should follow the teachings of Jesus Christ and the Bible. They wanted to convert the American Indians to Christianity. They believed only Christians went to heaven after death.

The Spanish sent Juan Rodríguez Cabrillo to explore the Alta California coast in 1542. He discovered the area that is now called San Diego Bay. Under Spanish rule, the name "Californias" described the part of Mexico that is now the Baja Peninsula and the land that is

Juan Rodríguez Cabrillo led the exploration into Alta California. ▶

Saint Louis, Bishop of Toulouse

Mission San Luis Obispo de Tolosa and the city of San Luis Obispo were named for Saint Louis, the Bishop of Toulouse. Toulouse is a city in the south of France. Born a prince in 1274, Louis was the son of Charles II, King of Naples, and the nephew of King Louis IX of France. Spanish soldiers kidnapped Louis and two of his brothers during a naval battle against Spain and held them ransom in exchange for their father. While they were captives in Spain, Catholic friars taught the boys. After seven years, the boys were released and Louis became a friar, giving up his claim to the throne. In 1296, he was appointed Bishop of Toulouse by Pope Boniface VIII, the top official of the Roman Catholic Church. Several months later, he caught a fever and died. He was 23. His feast day is celebrated on August 19th.

◀ *Saint Louis of Toulouse.*

now the state of California. The southern section of the Californias was called Baja (lower) California, while the northern section was called Alta (upper) California. Alta California eventually became the state of California.

Alta California

Baja California

New Spain

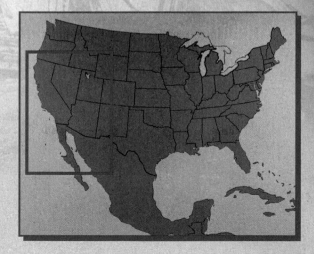

The Obispeño Chumash

Cabrillo saw many American Indians in his travels to Alta California. He traded cloth and beads with the Indians for food, such as berries and acorn bread. He wrote in his journals that the Indians were generous and peaceful. The Spanish hoped the Indians would welcome other explorers and settlers in the same way.

The Indians who lived in the San Luis Obispo area were mainly from the Chumash group. The Chumash Indians lived in several different tribal groups across a large part of Alta California. The Chumash who were associated with Mission San Luis Obispo de Tolosa are known as the Obispeño Chumash or Northern Chumash. A few Salinan Indians lived in the area, too. Although the Indians did not have a written history, much has been learned about the way they lived before the Spanish came to California in the 1700s. Historians and archeologists have pieced together information from stories the Chumash told from generation to generation and artifacts, like shell ornaments and stone bowls, that were found during excavations.

The Chumash culture was based on the natural world. The Chumash used items that they found in their environment for food, shelter, and protection. They learned from an early age how to be self-sufficient by gathering their own food and making their own tools and utensils.

Like other California Indians, the Chumash lived in small villages near rivers, streams, and the ocean. They were hunters and gatherers, which meant that they ate what animals, fish, and insects they could kill and what edible plants and nuts they could collect. They were free to move when their homes wore out. They could go off on hunting parties or live in temporary shelters while collecting acorn nuts. They could also

The Chumash Indians often hunted for food in the rivers near their villages. ▶

practice their own religion and ceremonies. They set their own schedule for living, which included much time for leisure.

The Chumash men did the hunting and fishing. They made weapons, traps, and snares to kill game, including deer, bear cubs, rabbits, squirrels, and birds. They fished in the nearby rivers and bays. The women gathered clams and other shellfish. On occasion, they ate whales that had come too close to shore and died.

The Chumash made tools from various objects they found in nature, including animal bones, shells, and rocks. They shaped spearheads and arrowheads out of rocks and minerals. One kind of stone they used for weapon tips was obsidian, which is like glass. Since obsidian wasn't available in their area, the Chumash traded with other Indian groups to get it. They used hard stones to form sharp edges on the obsidian until it was pointed and sharp enough to pierce an animal's skin. Some of the smaller pieces could be used like knife blades to carve animal bones and shells into fishing hooks, necklaces, and other items.

The Chumash women gathered much of the family's food and took care of the children. They gathered insects, acorns, piñon nuts, grass seeds, elderberries, and wild cherries (called *islay*) to eat. Acorns were an important source of nutrition for the Chumash. When the nuts didn't fall naturally from oak trees, the Chumash used sticks to shake the

Chumash women collected food in baskets like this one.

acorns down. Acorns could be stored for later use, so the Indians collected as many as possible in the fall months. The Chumash moved to temporary shelters near forests of oak trees in the fall. Certain lands belonged to them, and they sometimes fought with other groups that tried to gather food or hunt in their area. They collected the food in tightly woven baskets that they made from reeds. They used tule for mats and sandals and collected bunch grass for baskets. The women put tar on the insides of the baskets so they could carry water from the river.

The Chumash Indians lived in homes like these.

The Chumash built their homes in a domed shape. A hole in the roof let in fresh air and also let out smoke from fires used for cooking. The Chumash gathered willow for poles, then placed the poles in a large circle, bending them together to form a dome. After lashing the poles together and bracing them with smaller poles, they gathered tule to use as thatch, or roofing. They tied the tule down so it was tight enough to keep out rain. The Chumash left an opening for a doorway and made mats from tule to cover it.

Animal hides and tule were also used by the Chumash women for

13

The Marriage of Iseka

clothing. They made skirts from tule or strips of rabbit fur, decorated with shells. The Indian men wore little or no clothing at all. In cooler weather everyone wore animal furs draped over their shoulders for warmth. Both men and women wore their hair long. Sometimes the women decorated their hair with bands of shells.

The Chumash had special accessories that they wore for ceremonies, like beads, pendants, hair ornaments, and headdresses made of feathers, bone, stone, and shells. Some ceremony participants wore animal heads as hats and bear claws on a necklace. They often painted their bodies for rituals that included dancing and singing. The Chumash held ceremonies to acknowledge seasonal changes or solstices.

The Chumash religion was based on nature. They believed that plants, animals, and people could have special powers. For example, a bear's special power was its enormous strength. The Chumash believed in many gods (moon, sun, morning star, and earth). These gods could bring good and bad things. The Chumash wanted to please these gods, so they honored them with gifts and ceremonies. Medicine men, or shamans, healed the sick by chasing away evil spirits. The shamans used dancing, singing, and herbs as remedies.

◀ *This painting depicts the marriage of a Chumash couple.*

15

The Mission System

By the time the Spanish came to Alta California to build missions, they had already constructed similar settlements elsewhere in the New World. Beginning in the 1500s, Spanish soldiers, friars, and settlers traveled to Central America, South America, and Mexico to build religious settlements, or missions. They renamed the area that we now call Mexico "New Spain," in honor of their homeland. They set up their government headquarters and named this capital city Mexico City.

In New Spain, the religious settlements were built in areas where many Indians lived. The Spanish thought they could help the Indians by teaching them Christianity, European trades, and the Spanish language. They believed that the Indians were inferior to them and needed instruction. Some thought the Indians were "savages." The Spanish based their prejudices on the Indians' lifestyle. The Indians did not go to school, did not wear much clothing, painted their bodies, lived in rustic homes, and were not Christians. Because the Spanish had never seen such people before, they thought this way of life showed ignorance and a lack of culture, when in truth it was just a different culture from their own. The Spanish wanted the Indians to wear European clothing, which included shirts and trousers for the men and dresses for the women. They wanted the Indians to practice the Spanish religion and customs. The Spanish believed that this was in the best interest of the Indians. Today we have an appreciation for the value of different lifestyles and cultures. During this time in history, though, there was not as much respect for diversity.

Friars (called *frays* in Spanish) taught the Indians about the Spanish ways. In addition to farming, the friars showed the Indians how to care for livestock and how to become skilled in trades such as carpentry,

The Spanish did not understand the Chumash lifestyle. ▶

tanning, blacksmithing, weaving, soapmaking, and leathermaking. The friars also taught the Indians about the Christian god.

The soldiers worked with the friars in building the first settlement. The soldiers helped clear the land for building and planting. They also guarded it against threats from Indians who didn't want the Spanish people there and from other non-Spanish settlers who might come and try to take over the land. The soldiers built presidios (military fortresses) to keep the area safe from attack. Once the settlements were established and stable, settlers could come to the area and begin building towns and ranches.

The friars in Alta California followed the same plan. In both mission systems, the process of training the Indians and converting them to Christianity was supposed to take 10 years. After that time, the Indians could begin operating the mission lands as Spanish citizens who were required to pay taxes to the government. The intended process of returning the mission lands to the Christian Indians was called secularization. According to the plan, after a mission was secularized, the friars would start another settlement in a new location.

◄ *This European painting shows a friar teaching the Indians about Catholicism.*

The Beginnings of Mission San Luis Obispo de Tolosa

The Valley of the Bears

The Spanish sent more than 200 men from New Spain to start the mission chain in Alta California. The military leader was Captain Don Gaspár de Portolá. Of noble birth, Portolá began his military career in his youth and by the late 1760s had been named governor of the Californias. Fray Junípero Serra was sent to accompany Portolá as the president of the missions. A friar since 1737, Serra had operated missions in New Spain. Small in stature and often sickly, Serra almost didn't make the 750-mile journey to San Diego. Several years earlier, he had been bitten by an insect,

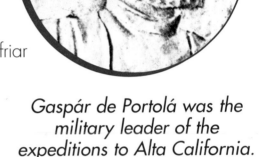

Gaspár de Portolá was the military leader of the expeditions to Alta California.

probably a mosquito, which had infected his leg and caused it to swell. It never healed and caused him much pain. He was determined to found the missions even though he had to be lifted onto a mule to make the trip. His motto was: "Always go forward. Never turn back."

Five expeditions (two by land and three by sea) left New Spain. Only four arrived in San Diego. One ship was lost at sea. The explorers planned to set up one mission in San Diego and another one 450 miles to the north, in Monterey. Portolá's expeditions included not only soldiers, sailors, and friars, but also Christian Indians from the missions in New Spain. The Spanish hoped the Indians could serve as translators. Only half of the group survived the journey. Some deserted,

Fray Junípero Serra went to Alta California as the president of the missions. ▶

while others got sick with scurvy, a disease caused by a lack of fresh fruits and vegetables.

While Fray Serra founded Mission San Diego de Alcalá on July 16, 1769, Portolá departed with 63 men in search of Monterey. The Monterey area had been explored in 1602 by Spanish explorer Sebastián Vizcaíno, who described it as a rich land of great beauty with much promise as a seaport. Portolá's group searched for Vizcaíno's Monterey but could not find it. Tired and hungry, Portolá and his men decided to head back to San Diego. They were desperate for food when they entered a swampy valley surrounded by eroding hillsides. They noticed that much of the soil was overturned and soon realized that grizzly bears had dug it up searching for roots to eat. One bear nearly killed them before they used their guns to slay it. They killed more bears to eat. The Spanish called the land La Cañada de los Osos, which means the "Valley of the Bears."

A short time later, the Spanish found Monterey and established Mission San Carlos Borromeo del Río Carmelo. They also began a third settlement south of Monterey called Mission San Antonio de Padua. These new missions were in their infancy and struggling to survive when they experienced a severe food shortage. Portolá sent an expedition back to the Valley of the Bears to hunt. In three months, the group collected 9,000 pounds of meat, which saved the residents of Mission San Carlos Borromeo and Mission San Antonio from starvation. The expedition also traded with the Chumash Indians for seeds and other foods. The Indians were fascinated by the Spanish guns. The Chumash could not kill grizzlies with arrows alone. On occasion, they

◀ *Don Gaspár de Portolá's group entered the Valley of the Bears tired and hungry.*

ate bear meat, but it was usually from cubs they had caught.

The Spanish thought that the area, which was rich with game and water and had a mild climate, would make a good site for a mission. They also found the Chumash to be friendly and helpful. On September 1, 1772, Fray Serra came to the Valley of the Bears and picked a spot for a new mission. Among the men who accompanied Serra was Pedro Fages, who had taken command of the military after Portolá returned to New Spain in 1770. The men planted a cross in the ground near a stream. Fray Serra performed a Catholic church service called Mass and founded Mission San Luis Obispo de Tolosa.

Starting the Mission

After the founding ceremony at Mission San Luis Obispo in 1772, Fray Serra and others in the expedition needed to check on supplies at Mission San Diego de Alcalá. After this expedition left, only eight men remained to begin building the mission. Fray José Cavaller was named the head missionary. Five soldiers and two Christian Indians made up the rest of the small group. The group had brought three mules, some farming tools, and some church items to be used at the mission. Usually missions had two friars to operate them, but Cavaller was the only friar at Mission San Luis Obispo for many years.

The men had other supplies, such as sugar, flour, chocolate, and wheat, and later, more arrived by ship. The Spanish planned to trade some of their goods with the Chumash for seeds and other useful items. Fray Serra knew that leaving so few men was a risky decision, but he was eager to continue converting the Indians of California to the

Some Indians were forced to convert against their will.

Christian faith. He wrote in his journal that God "would not abandon the agents of so holy an enterprise." He meant that he believed God would watch over the missionaries.

Fray Cavaller and the others had much work to do. First they needed to construct temporary shelters, including a church and living quarters. They cut tree boughs and lashed them together to form a stockade. They were thankful to receive help from the Chumash. In fact, the travelers from Spain

would not have survived their first year in Alta California without the hospitality of the Chumash.

The Indians contributed for several reasons. The Spanish and the Chumash at San Luis Obispo had established good relations by sharing food with each other in the past. The Chumash supplied seeds, while the Spanish offered bear meat. The Chumash wanted to help the Spanish because the Spanish had fabrics, tools, and trinkets that they had never seen before. The Spanish had tools made out of metal, which intrigued the Chumash. The soldiers and missionaries used these items to attract the Indians to the mission. Some of the Indians wanted to try the Spanish tools and offered to help. Once the Indians came to assist, the Spanish urged them to stay. Attracting converts to the mission was slow in the early years, as the Chumash could obtain the food and materials they needed to survive without the help of the Spanish. However, some wanted to become Christians and were baptized. (Baptism is a ceremony that is held when someone accepts the Christian faith. A converted Indian was called a neophyte.)

By 1805, 33 years after its founding, the mission population peaked at 961 neophytes. Once they converted to Christianity, the Chumash were required to live at the mission and were not allowed to leave without the friars' permission. The Spanish allowed the Indians to return to their former villages from time to time. They hoped that the Chumash would bring friends and relatives back to the mission. The friars allowed one-fifth of the group to leave each week, so an Indian could return to his or her village once every five weeks. However, those who lived at the mission lost the freedom they had once had to roam the land when

◀ *Indians were baptized when they were accepted into the Christian faith.*

they wanted, because they were now needed to help run the mission complex and to care for the crops and livestock.

Building and Rebuilding the Mission

The missionaries, soldiers, and Chumash began to build more permanent structures later in the 1770s. They gathered supplies from the valley and surrounding area. They needed wood to build the dwellings. Alta California had many forests of oak, pine, and redwood trees. After cutting the trees into planks and posts, the workers used these pieces to make supports for the buildings. To move the lumber from place to place, they used small carts that the Spanish called *carretas*.

Though wooden structures were the easiest and fastest to build, the Spanish knew such buildings were dangerous because they

Neophytes learned how to make adobe.

Adobe was packed into molds and left to dry in the sun.

caught fire very quickly. They decided to reconstruct the buildings out of adobe brick. The Spanish showed the Chumash how to make adobe out of mud, straw, and water. Sometimes the workers used their feet to mix it up, or they used animals to stomp it together. They packed the adobe into wooden molds and then left the bricks to dry in the sun. Once the

The bricks were stacked on top of one another and held together with mud.

bricks hardened, they were ready to be used to form walls.

Since making the bricks was time consuming, the mission took many years to build. Initially, the roofs of mission buildings were made of poles lashed together and covered with tule, but the roofs were burned in three separate incidents when Mission San Luis Obispo was attacked by Indians. The fire spread to other buildings, destroying some of the living quarters, food supplies, tools, and other materials. The Indians who attacked the mission had a disagreement with one of the Indians living at Mission San Luis Obispo over the intentions of the Spanish missionaries. Believing that the Spanish were trespassing, these Indians didn't want to adopt the Christian religion or learn European trade skills. They liked their lifestyle the way it was before the missionaries came. However, the Chumash living at the mission helped put out the fires and began rebuilding the mission. The missionaries were determined to stay.

To make the roofs fire-resistant at Mission San Luis Obispo, the mission friars covered the roofs with clay tiles, called *tejas,* which wouldn't burn as easily. They showed the Chumash how to make these from clay and water. They also made floor tiles, called *ladrillos,* out of clay. Soon, other missions began making tiles for their roofs to prevent fires.

As the mission's neophyte population grew, so did the mission complex. Eventually it was expanded to contain dormitories (called *monjerios*) for single Indian girls and women, soldiers' barracks, storerooms, workrooms, mills, a granary, a hospital, and Indian houses. It also included miles of aqueducts, which supplied water to the community and gardens, outlying *ranchos* (farms), and two *asistencias* (branch churches).

This picture of the mission is from 1875.

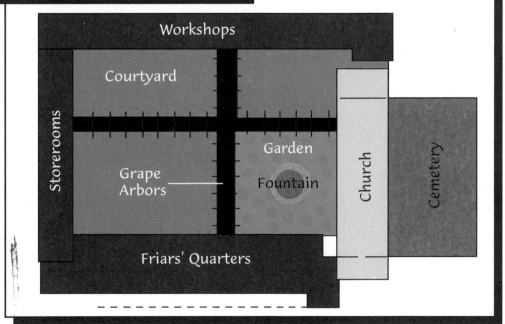

This is the floor plan of Mission San Luis Obispo de Tolosa.

Daily Life at the Mission

Life at the mission presented difficulties for everyone living there. The friars set the daily schedule and made sure everyone followed it. Mission life was highly structured, and there was little time for leisure. This new lifestyle provided much less freedom than the Chumash had before the Spanish came into their land and lives. Many Chumash had trouble adapting to the Spanish lifestyle.

Most missions in Alta California followed the same daily schedule. The day began around sunrise when the mission's residents were awakened by bells. They gathered and headed to the church for Mass, morning prayers, and church lessons. After church came breakfast. The Indians were served a mush made of grain or corn, called *atole*.

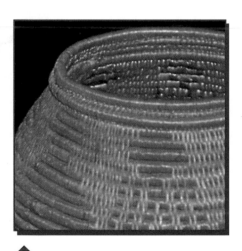

▲
The Chumash women made baskets.

Then the residents went to work. There were many jobs at the mission, some for men and others for women. The Chumash men were responsible for farming, ranching, leathermaking, ironworking, tanning, carpentry, and construction. The Chumash women cooked the food and made baskets and soap. The Spanish showed them how to weave using European looms. The women made clothing for the friars, soldiers, and Chumash living at the mission. They also wove blankets. The friars showed the Indians how to do many of these things, but sometimes skilled craftsmen were brought in from missions in New Spain to instruct.

32

The Chumash learned Spanish farming methods at the mission. ▶

Many missionaries worked side by side with the Indians.

At Mission San Luis Obispo, the Chumash raised livestock, including sheep, cattle, mules, and horses. They planted wheat, fruit trees, corn, beans, and other vegetables. They grew grapes to make wine and olives to make olive oil. The Chumash women began using corn and wheat flours instead of acorn flour. They still collected nuts and edible plants, especially in the early years of the mission system before much farming had begun.

After the morning work session ended, the laborers had lunch. They were served a soup called *pozole*, that was made of grain, vegetables, and meat. After lunch they took a rest, called a *siesta*. A short period of work followed in the afternoon. Then everyone gathered again for Mass, dinner, which usually included *atole*, and prayers. More church instruction was held in the evenings, as well as Spanish language lessons. Then there was a little time for leisure. Although the friars frowned upon it, the Indians liked to gamble. The Chumash also enjoyed singing and dancing.

Sometimes the daily routine varied. The Spanish liked to hold *fiestas*, or festivals, honoring various saints, important events in church history, births, and weddings. The Indians wanted to practice their traditional ceremonies, too. These rituals were contrary to Catholic teachings and were discouraged by the friars. However, many pretended not to notice these Indian rituals because they wanted the Indians to remain peaceful and stay at the mission to learn about Christianity.

Mission life was challenging for the soldiers and friars. Many experienced a feeling of isolation being so far away from loved ones

◀ *The Chumash women learned to cook with corn and wheat flours instead of acorn flour.*

and their homeland. In addition, they had to adjust to a different environment, climate, and style of living. There were few comforts at the mission and there were many food shortages. Their living quarters were rustic, with dirt floors, wooden cots, and scratchy blankets. The food was often bland.

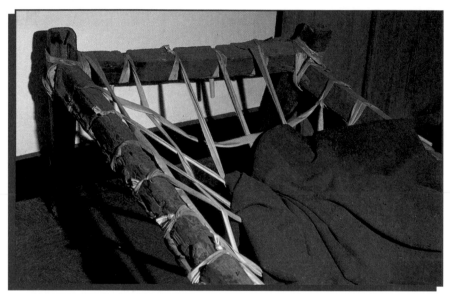

▲

The mission beds were rustic and small.

The missionaries had many jobs to do. They taught the neophytes about farming, ranching, crafts, and religion. They prepared religious lessons and performed church services, weddings, funerals, and baptisms. Since the missions were under the authority of the government in New Spain, the missionaries also had to deal with a lot of official business. They were required to write yearly reports, keeping records of life at the missions. In 1803, the friars at Mission San Luis Obispo recorded 239 new neophytes living at the mission. In 1832, records show 5,422 sheep, 2,500 cattle, 700 horses, and 200 mules. The friars also noted a total of 763 marriages, 2,268

▲

The friars' duties included leading religious ceremonies.

deaths, and 2,644 baptisms in a 60-year span. Such records are what allow historians today to understand the productivity of each mission.

Hardships at the Mission

Conflict

Many factors contributed to the conflict between the California Indians and the Spanish soldiers and missionaries. While many of the Indians may have converted to Christianity and moved to the missions because they believed in the religion, some only came because the Spanish provided food, shelter, and access to new tools. Some neophytes quickly became frustrated and unhappy. Sometimes they stole from the mission and were punished. Once the Indians were living at the mission, they were not allowed to leave without the missionaries' permission. If the Indians tried to escape, they were rounded up, brought back to the mission, and punished in front of the other neophytes. This was meant to discourage other Indians from trying to leave.

Fray Serra.

Many Spanish soldiers were brutal in their treatment of the neophytes. Pedro Fages, who was in charge of the military after Portolá left Alta California in 1770, even treated his own soldiers harshly. He was a young man and was inexperienced in dealing with mission settlements. He was rigid with his soldiers, who were often lazy, rude, and disorderly. They didn't want to work, but they helped themselves to mission food and other goods. Some were very cruel, severely beating and mistreating the Indians.

Fray Serra didn't get along with Pedro Fages. Fages thought the military should

At some missions, the neophytes were punished when they didn't attend church. ▶

govern the missions, while Serra thought the friars should. Fages wouldn't change his mind, so Serra returned to New Spain in the early 1770s to ask the government to remove Fages as military head of Alta California. Serra was successful. He obtained a document from the government stating that the missionaries could take the control of the Indians away from the military. At the time, this document was considered a Native American Bill of Rights, though many soldiers disregarded it and continued the abuse.

The soldiers' treatment of the Indians only fueled the anger of the Chumash who didn't want the missionaries on their lands, forcing them to adopt a new lifestyle and religion. They attacked Mission San Luis Obispo several times but found their arrows were no match for the Spanish guns.

To ease relations, the missionaries allowed the neophytes to choose an Indian to be an *alcalde*, beginning in 1780. *Alcaldes* acted as go-betweens for the neophytes and the friars. Their job was to keep the peace by making sure each side was represented and each side was understood by the other.

Death and Disease

The Spanish arrival in New Spain and eventually in Alta California exposed the American Indians to many European diseases that they had never had contact with before. Their bodies had not built up any resistance to chicken pox, measles, smallpox, or syphilis. Diseases like these took their toll on the mission's population, and many Chumash died.

Many of the Chumash, especially single girls and women, lived in cramped quarters. The adobe bricks kept the *monjeríos* cool and

◀ *Many of the Chumash were unhappy at the mission.*

41

damp. The humid air made breathing difficult for some people and many became very sick. In addition, the poor sanitation systems in the dormitories attracted bugs and rats. These creatures brought even more sickness and death to the Chumash who lived there.

Changes at the Mission

Despite its problems, Mission San Luis Obispo continued to grow. In 1789, Fray Cavaller died and was buried beneath the floor of the mission's church. He was replaced by Fray Miguel Giribet, who was joined eight years later by Fray Luis Antonio Martínez. Martínez was a friendly, jolly man who was able to establish good relations with the Chumash. He was also known for his odd antics. One story claims that when a general and his wife visited the mission, Fray Martínez had all the poultry in the barnyard assembled and paraded past the guests. However, he had less success in winning over the military. He often thought soldiers were too lazy, and because he was quick-tempered he would easily speak his mind.

Fray Martínez did manage to impress the soldiers when South American pirates attacked several of the missions. He led a group of mission Chumash to defend the settlements at Santa Bárbara and San Juan Capistrano.

War in Mexico

In 1810, the people in New Spain declared war on Spain. They wanted to gain their independence from the Spanish. Previously, the government in New Spain had sent money and supplies to help the missions grow, but now these goods were kept for the war. Mission San Luis Obispo somehow still managed to prosper.

In 1821, the people in New Spain gained their independence from Spain. They formed the new nation of Mexico. Alta California and the missions there now belonged to Mexico. Three years later the neophytes at Missions Santa Bárbara, La Purísima, and Santa Inés revolted against the mission system, but the San Luis Obispo Chumash did not.

Although the neophytes at Mission San Luis Obispo did not revolt, this mission had its own troubles. Tensions between Fray Martínez and the military reached a breaking point in 1830. He was banished from Alta California on charges of treason. That same year an earthquake rocked the mission, causing severe damage to the buildings.

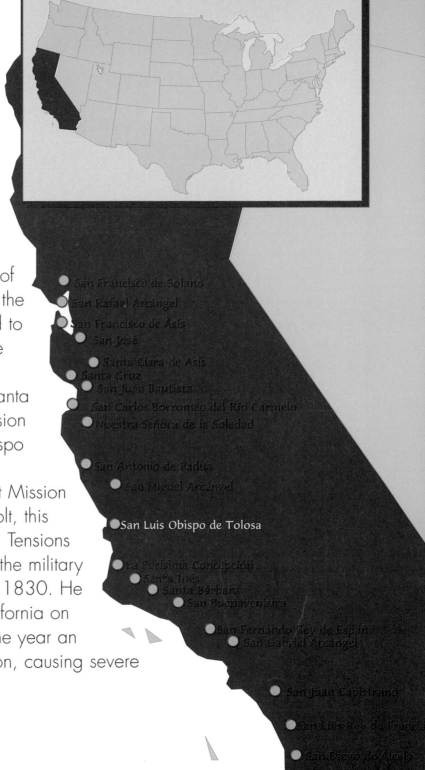

San Francisco de Solano
San Rafael Arcángel
San Francisco de Asís
San José
Santa Clara de Asís
Santa Cruz
San Juan Bautista
San Carlos Borromeo del Río Carmelo
Nuestra Señora de la Soledad
San Antonio de Padua
San Miguel Arcángel
San Luis Obispo de Tolosa
La Purísima Concepción
Santa Inés
Santa Bárbara
San Buenaventura
San Fernando Rey de España
San Gabriel Arcángel
San Juan Capistrano
San Luis Rey de Francia
San Diego de Alcalá

Secularization and Statehood in California

When they began the mission system, the Spanish had planned to secularize the missions after 10 years of operation, but they didn't. The friars had asked for more time because they didn't think the Indians were ready to operate the missions without them. Once Mexico gained its independence from Spain, Alta California and its missions were governed by the Mexicans. Mexico finally decided to secularize the missions in the 1830s. Some Mexicans said that the Indians were being treated like slaves at the missions. Others wanted to take over the rich mission lands to become wealthy.

The Mexicans passed secularization laws in August 1833. These laws took the control of the missions away from the Franciscans and gave it to the Mexican government. The government was supposed to redistribute the land to the converted Indians and other residents of the mission settlements, but instead most of the mission property was given as gifts to favored people of influence. Some of the mission Indians received small plots of land in and around the mission area. Many Indians left the mission to find work elsewhere or to return to their villages. Unfortunately, many Indian villages no longer existed. Ranchers and settlers had taken them over. Some Chumash found jobs as servants and as *vaqueros* (cowboys or ranch hands) on nearby ranches. Others formed small settlements in the outlying areas.

Most Indians never received any of the mission lands. Instead, the land was sold by corrupt Mexican officials or taken over by Americans and other immigrant settlers. In 1845, Governor Pio Pico sold what was left of Mission San Luis Obispo, except for the church, to Captain John Wilson and his partners, McKinley and Scott, for $510.

Mission San Luis Obispo de Tolosa. ▶

▲

Secularization left the mission in poor condition.

After it was sold, Mission San Luis Obispo gradually fell apart. An earthquake left most of the adobe structures in ruins. There were too few Indians left to repair the structures. Some of the buildings that were still usable were rented out and used as a jail, school, and courthouse.

The political instability in Alta California continued. Americans were moving into the territory, and soon war broke out between Mexico and the United States. On one occasion, United States captain John C. Frémont received a report that Mexican rebels had taken over Mission San Luis Obispo. His troops surrounded the complex and prepared to fight. Instead of Mexican soldiers, Frémont's men found a few women and children inside, seeking shelter.

After the Americans won the war, Alta California became part of the United States. In 1850, Alta California became the state of California. Miners and settlers had flocked to the area after gold was discovered in Coloma, California, in the late 1840s. These new settlers were cruel to the Indians. The American settlers pushed the Indians off their lands. Finally, the United States government designated certain lands, called reservations, which the Indians could live on without disturbance. Unfortunately, many of these reservations offered only poor living conditions.

In 1859, the settlement that had grown around Mission San Luis Obispo officially became a town. By 1872, the mission was in extremely bad shape, so the Catholic community (who had been returned a small portion of the mission lands in 1859) raised money to put up a shingled roof and add a steeple to the church. Southern Pacific Railroad built tracks through the area in 1894, which made travel to the town much easier. Thanks to the restored church and the new train line, the town began to grow.

The Mission Today

In the 1930s, Father Harnett, a parish friar, began efforts to have the mission restored to the way it looked in the late 1700s. Today, Mission San Luis Obispo serves as a church and a community center, as well as a historical site. Visitors come from all over the world to get a glimpse of how the early Californians lived.

The mission contains a museum that is decorated with Indian symbols and drawings. Sketches and photographs of the mission line the museum walls. The museum also houses the largest collection of American Indian artifacts of any of the California missions. The exhibit cases are filled with grinding stones, tools, and shell ornaments. Other exhibits include European tools, looms, furniture, and wine vats.

▲

Chumash art decorates the museum at Mission San Luis Obispo.

Today, San Luis Obispo calls itself the City with a Mission. The influences of the Spanish friars and Chumash Indians can still be seen. A few Chumash continue to weave baskets in the style of their ancestors. Vineyards and wineries fill the landscape of San Luis Obispo County, helping to make California a leading producer of wines that are famous throughout the world.

Today, Mission San Luis Obispo is an important part of the community. ▶

1772

MISSION

SAN LUIS OBISPO de TOLOSA

MASSES

SUNDAYS: SATURDAY EVENING 5:30 PM
SUNDAY 7 , 9:00, 10:30 A.M., 12:00 NOON AND 6:00 PM

HOLY DAYS: EVENING PRIOR 5:30 PM
HOLY DAY 7:00, 8:00 A.M., 12:00 NOON, 5:30

WEEK DAYS: 7:00, 8 A.M. AND 5:30 PM

SACRAMENT OF PENANCE

SATURDAYS, AND EVES of HOLY DAYS

Mission San Luis Obispo's vineyards help make California one of the leading wine producers in the world.

With its parish church, youth center, and senior center, Mission San Luis Obispo is still the core of activity in this city, and the hard work and struggle of its founders are remembered today.

The Church and Its Artwork

The church at Mission San Luis Obispo has brightly colored designs on the walls and ceiling. The bright red ceiling beams are linked by small white planks, which feature small, blue, eight-pointed stars. The friars and the Chumash painted the designs with paints they made. They mixed pigments made from natural materials found in the area, such as iron ore (red), yellow clay (yellow), and charcoal (black), with cactus juice or linseed oil. Indigo, a plant with a bright blue flower, was brought from Spain to make the color blue.

The church contains many paintings and sculptures of the

saints. Above the altar in the church at Mission San Luis Obispo hangs a painting of Saint Louis. Although the work is not signed, art historians believe it was painted by José de Páez, an artist who did a lot of work for the California missions in the late 1700s. The painting shows Saint Louis dressed in a red cloak, holding a shepherd's staff, and wearing a large cross on a chain around his neck. On the ground next to his feet are a crown and scepter. This is symbolic of Saint Louis' choice to become a friar rather than king.

◀ *This statue of Saint Louis stands in the mission.*

Make Your Own Mission
San Luis Obispo

To make your own model of the San Luis Obispo de Padua mission, you will need:

cardboard
toiletpaper rolls
Scotch tape (or wood glue)
red beads

white paint
glue
green construction paper
Styrofoam
toothpicks

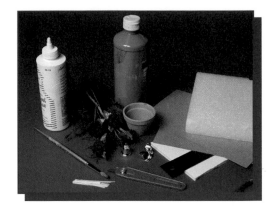

Directions

Step 1: Glue green construction paper to a large piece of cardboard. This will be the base for your model.

Step 2: To make the church walls, cut three 4" by 8" pieces of cardboard for the sides and back. Cut a 4" by 4" piece for the roof.

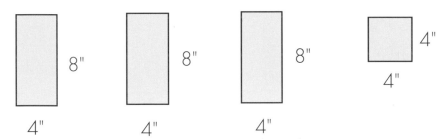

Adult supervision is suggested.

Step 3: Cut a 6" by 11" cardboard piece for the church front. Cut arched doors and windows. Cut the top so it is triangular.

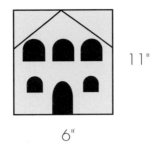

11"

6"

Step 4: Glue a toothpick behind each of the three windows. Use wire to attach a bell to each toothpick. Make a cross out of toothpicks and glue it to the top of the church front.

Step 5: Tape the sides, front, back, and roof of the church together. Paint the church white and let it dry.

Step 6: Glue the mission church to the base.

Step 7: To make the quadrangle buildings, cut four 10" by 4" cardboard pieces. Paint them white and let them dry.

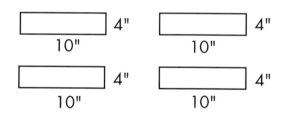

Step 8: Tape the quadrangle walls together in a square and place the square next to the church on the base.

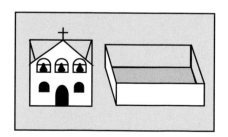

Step 9: Cut two 10″ by 4″ pieces of cardboard for the roofing of the quadrangle buildings.

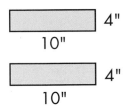

4″
10″

4″
10″

Step 10: Glue red beads to the top of both of the roof pieces.

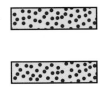

Step 11: Glue a roof panel on top of the back wall of the quadrangle. Place a toilet paper roll under it inside the courtyard for extra support.

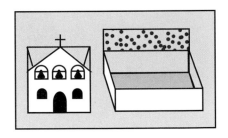

Step 12: Place the second roof panel on top of the front wall of the mission quadrangle. Place a toilet paper roll under it for extra support.

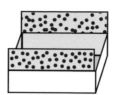

Step 13: Paint the toilet paper rolls and wrap them in fake leaves to make them look like trees in the courtyard.

Step 14: Paint windows on the outside walls of the quadrangle buildings.

Step 15: Decorate the mission grounds with crosses, trees, and flowers.

*Use the above mission as a reference for building your mission.

Important Dates in Mission History

1492	Christopher Columbus reaches the West Indies
1542	Cabrillo's expedition to California
1602	Sebastián Vizcaíno sails to California
1713	Fray Junípero Serra is born
1769	Founding of San Diego de Alcalá
1770	Founding of San Carlos Borromeo del Río Carmelo
1771	Founding of San Antonio de Padua and San Gabriel Arcángel
1772	**Founding of San Luis Obispo de Tolosa**
1775–76	Founding of San Juan Capistrano
1776	Founding of San Francisco de Asís
1776	Declaration of Independence is signed
1777	Founding of Santa Clara de Asís
1782	Founding of San Buenaventura
1784	Fray Serra dies
1786	Founding of Santa Bárbara Virgen y Mártir
1787	Founding of La Purísima Concepción de Maria Santísima
1791	Founding of Santa Cruz and Nuestra Señora de la Soledad
1797	Founding of San José, San Juan Bautista, San Miguel Arcángel, and San Fernando Rey de España
1798	Founding of San Luis Rey de Francia
1804	Founding of Santa Inés Virgen y Mártir
1817	Founding of San Rafael Arcángel
1823	Founding of San Francisco de Solano
1849	Gold found in northern California
1850	California becomes the 31st state

Glossary

adobe (uh-DOH-bee) Sun-dried bricks made of straw, mud, and sometimes manure.

Alta California (AL-tuh kal-ih-FOR-nya) An area known today as the state of California.

Baja California (BAH-ha kal-ih-FOR-nya) The Mexican peninsula directly south of the state of California.

baptize (BAP-tyz) A Christian ceremony to cleanse someone of his/her sins.

Christian (KRIS-chun) A person who follows the teachings of Jesus Christ and the Bible.

convert (CON-vert) Someone who has changed religious beliefs.

granary (GRAY-nuh-ree) A place to store grain.

ritual (RIH-choo-wul) A religious ceremony.

secularization (sehk-yoo-luh-rih-ZAY-shun) A process by which the mission lands were to be made non-religious.

thatch (THACH) Roofing made of twigs, grass, and bark bundled together.

Pronunciation Guide

alcaldes (ahl-KAHL-days)

asistencias (ah-sis-TEN-see-uhs)

atole (ah-TOH-lay)

La Cañada de los Osos (LAH cahn-YAH-dah DAY LOHS OH-sohs)

carretas (kah-RAY-tas)

fiesta (fee-EHS-tah)

fray (FRAY)

islay (EES-lay)

ladrillos (lah-DREE-yohs)

monjeríos (mohn-HAYR-ee-ohz)

pozole (poh-ZOH-lay)

ranchos (RAHN-chohs)

siesta (see-EHS-tah)

tejas (TAY-hahs)

vaqueros (bah-KEH-rohs)

Resources

For more information on the missions of California, check out these books and Web sites:

Books:
Bleeker, Sonia. *The Mission Indians of California*. New York: William Morrow and Company, 1956.

Giffords, Gloria. *Spanish Colonial Missions*. Southwest Parks and Monument Association, 1988.

Lyngheim, Linda. *The Indians and the California Missions*. Van Nuys, CA: Langtry Publications, 1990.

White, Florence Meiman. *The Story of Junípero Serra, Brave Adventurer*. New York: Parachute Press, Inc., 1987.

Web Sites:
Newhall Elementary Cyber Serra Virtual Mission Tour
http://www.newhall.k12.ca.us/newhall/cyberserra/cyberserra.htm

Index